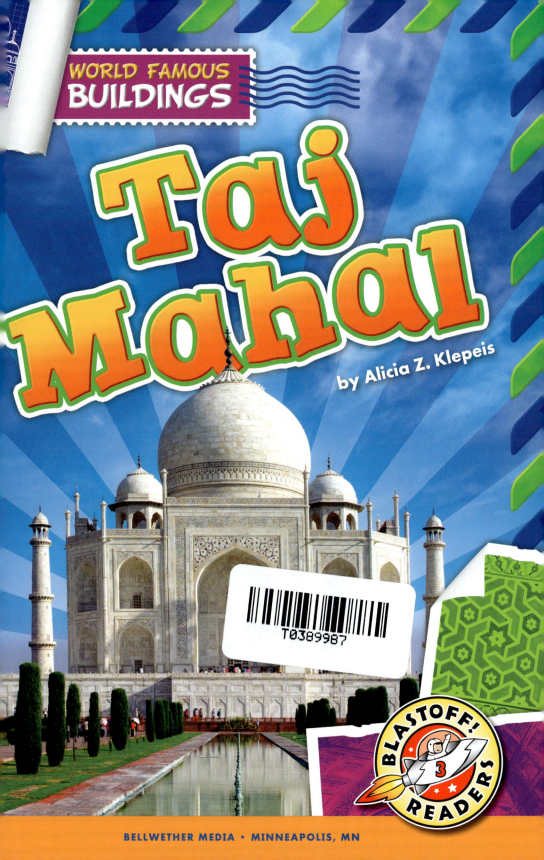

Blastoff! Readers are carefully developed by literacy experts to build reading stamina and move students toward fluency by combining standards-based content with developmentally appropriate text.

Level 1 provides the most support through repetition of high-frequency words, light text, predictable sentence patterns, and strong visual support.

Level 2 offers early readers a bit more challenge through varied sentences, increased text load, and text-supportive special features.

Level 3 advances early-fluent readers toward fluency through increased text load, less reliance on photos, advancing concepts, longer sentences, and more complex special features.

★ **Blastoff! Universe**

This edition first published in 2026 by Bellwether Media, Inc.

No part of this publication may be reproduced in whole or in part without written permission of the publisher. For information regarding permission, write to Bellwether Media, Inc., Attention: Permissions Department, 3500 American Blvd W, Suite 150, Bloomington, MN 55431.

Library of Congress Cataloging-in-Publication Data

LC record for Taj Mahal available at: https://lccn.loc.gov/2025021811

Text copyright © 2026 by Bellwether Media, Inc. BLASTOFF! READERS and associated logos are trademarks and/or registered trademarks of Bellwether Media, Inc. Bellwether Media is a division of FlutterBee Education Group.

Editor: Megan Borgert-Spaniol   Series Designer: Chase Demmin

Printed in the United States of America, North Mankato, MN.

Table of Contents

What Is the Taj Mahal?	4
History of the Taj Mahal	8
Parts of the Taj Mahal	14
The Taj Mahal Today	18
Glossary	22
To Learn More	23
Index	24

What Is the Taj Mahal?

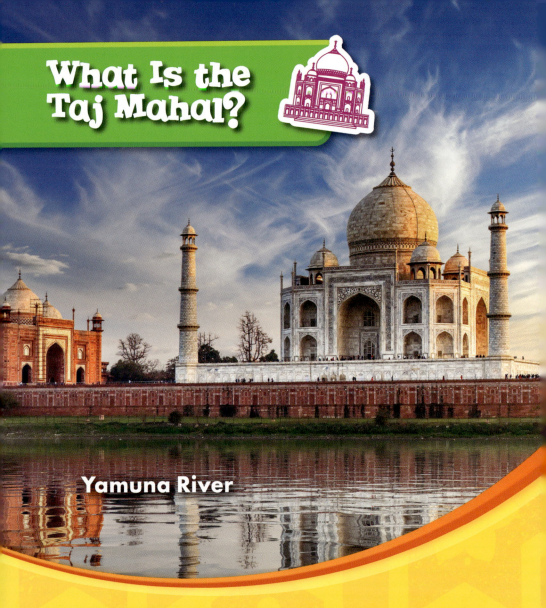

Yamuna River

The Taj Mahal is a famous **mausoleum**. *Taj Mahal* means "crown palace."

The Taj Mahal is in Agra, India. It stands along the Yamuna River.

Building Location

Agra, India

The Taj Mahal's marble **exterior** stands out.
It looks pink at sunrise.
It looks white during the day.
It looks golden at sunset.
It looks silver at night!

Visitors enjoy the building's **reflecting pool**.

History of the Taj Mahal

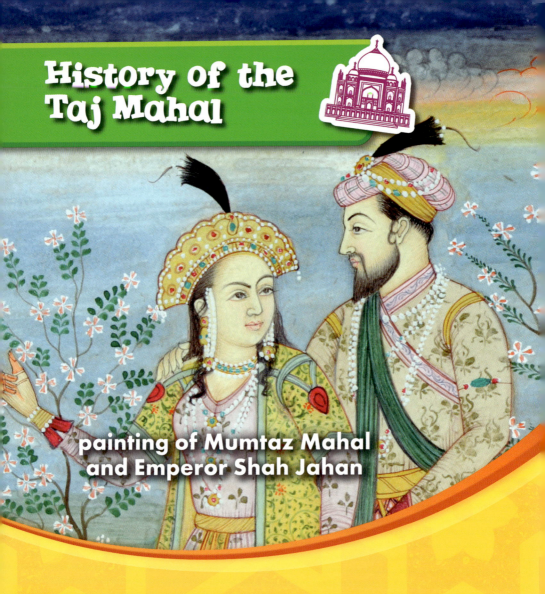

painting of Mumtaz Mahal and Emperor Shah Jahan

The Taj Mahal was built to honor Mumtaz Mahal. She died in 1631. She was the wife of **Emperor** Shah Jahan.

Workers began building it in 1632. They finished it in 1648. The main **architect** was Ustad Ahmad Lahori.

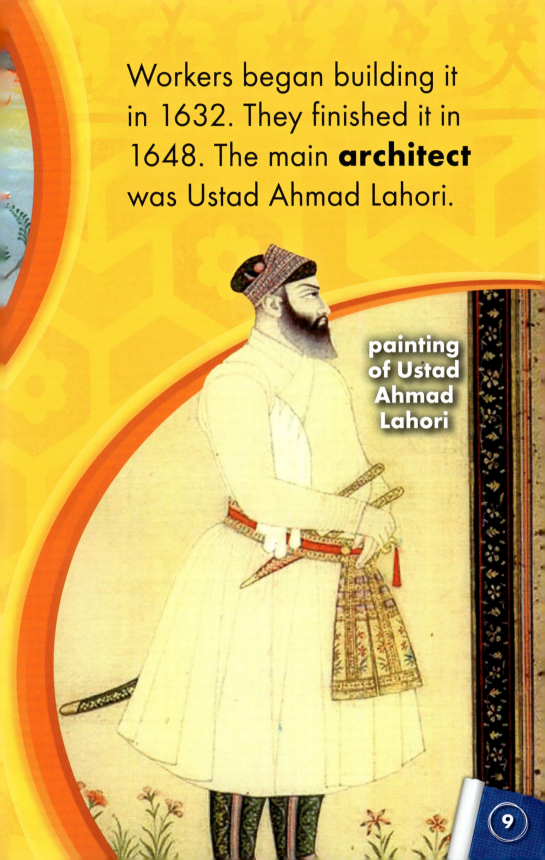

painting of Ustad Ahmad Lahori

More than 1,000 elephants carried building supplies to the site.

Workers dug wells into the ground. They filled the wells with stone. This made a strong **foundation**. A red sandstone platform was built over it.

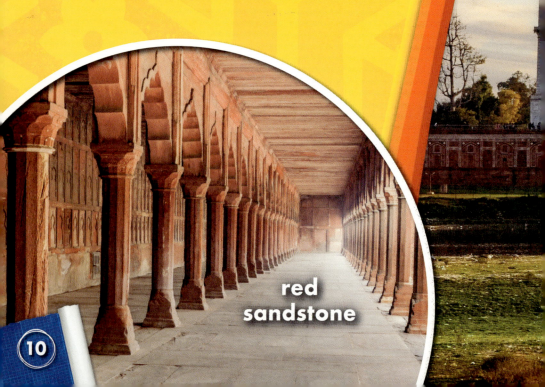

red sandstone

Workers built the mausoleum out of brick. Then they covered it with white marble. Gemstones were added to the marble.

gemstones

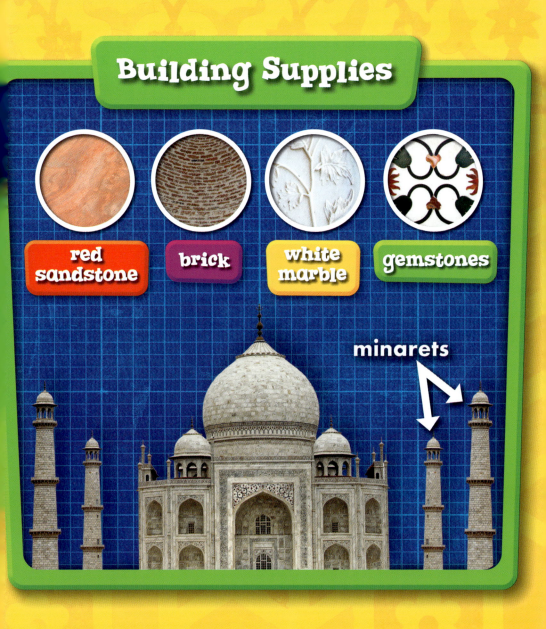

Four marble **minarets** were built around the mausoleum.

Parts of the Taj Mahal

The Taj Mahal is 240 feet (73 meters) high. Its main **dome** is onion-shaped. Four smaller domes surround it.

The building has many arches. Some arches have **calligraphy**. It has passages from the **Qur'an**.

domes

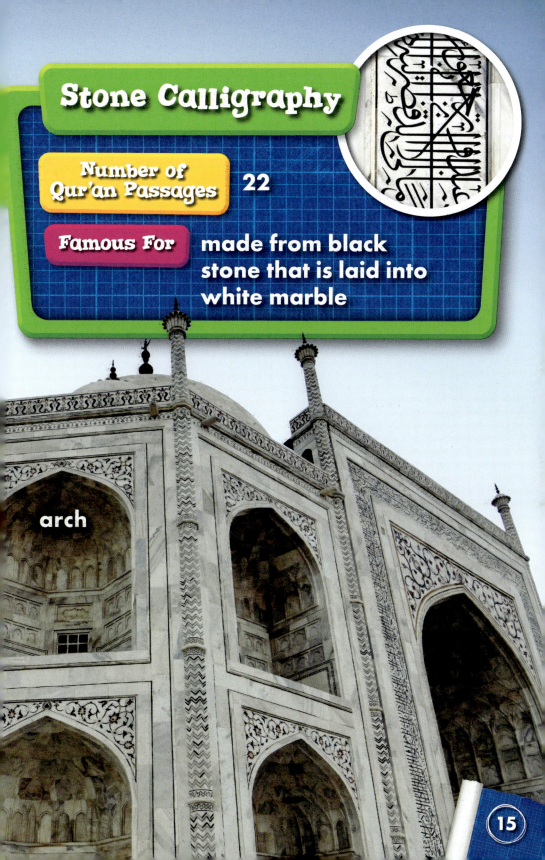

Stone Calligraphy

Number of Qur'an Passages: 22

Famous For: made from black stone that is laid into white marble

arch

Buildings sit on either side of the mausoleum. One is a **mosque**. The other is a guesthouse.

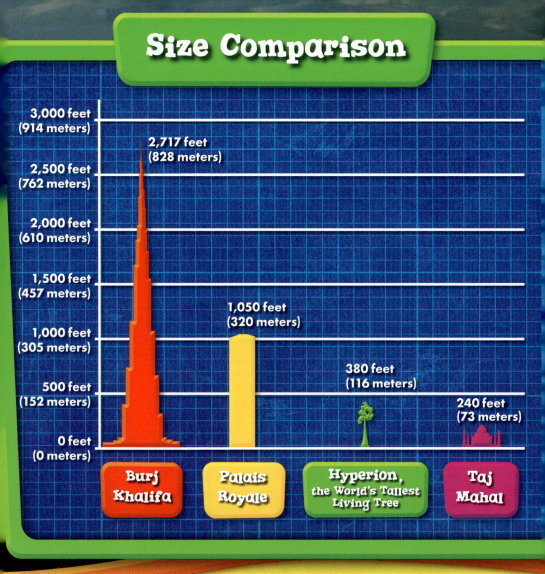

They look the same on the outside. Both are made of red sandstone.

The Taj Mahal Today

marble of the Taj Mahal dirty from pollution

The Taj Mahal draws millions of visitors each year. But **pollution** from factories and cars makes the building dirty.

Leaders have closed factories. They try to keep cars away. These changes help stop pollution.

Workers also clean the Taj Mahal's marble. They use a special clay. It helps remove dirt from the marble.

This care will help the Taj Mahal shine for a long time!

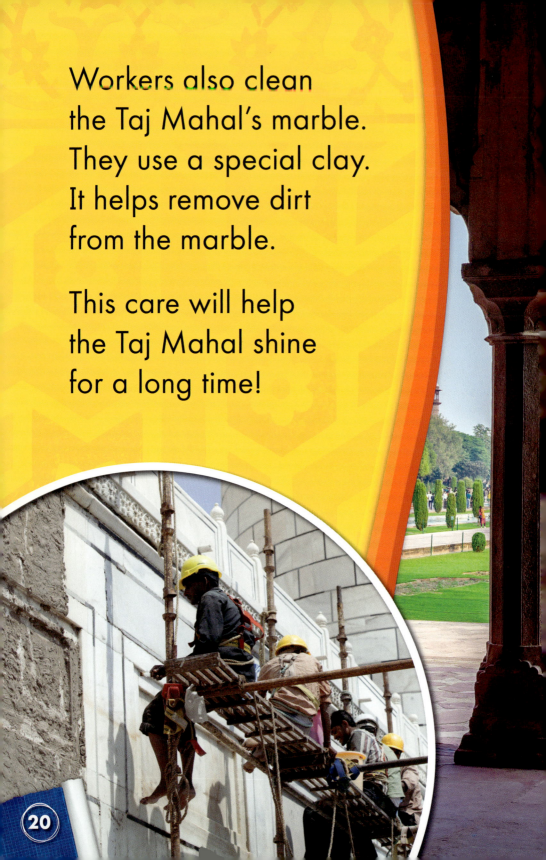

Glossary

architect—a person who plans and designs buildings

calligraphy—an artistic style of handwriting or lettering

dome—a structure with a rounded top and a circular base; a dome looks like half of a ball.

emperor—ruler

exterior—the outside of a building

foundation—the base or support on which a building rests

mausoleum—a tomb or building where someone is buried

minarets—tall, thin towers attached to a mosque; minarets have balconies used to call people to prayers.

mosque—a building that Muslims use for worship; Muslims are followers of the Islamic faith.

pollution—substances that make the earth dirty or unsafe

Qur'an—the holy book of Islam

reflecting pool—a pool of water that reflects its surroundings; a reflection is the return of light or sound waves from a surface.

To Learn More

AT THE LIBRARY
Bolte, Mari. *Taj Mahal.* Mankato, Minn.: Creative Education, 2025.

Gish, Ashley. *Taj Mahal.* Lake Elmo, Minn.: Focus Readers, 2023.

Rajan, Rekha S. *Amazing Landmarks.* New York, N.Y.: Scholastic Press, 2022.

ON THE WEB

FACTSURFER

Factsurfer.com gives you a safe, fun way to find more information.

1. Go to www.factsurfer.com.

2. Enter "Taj Mahal" into the search box and click 🔍.

3. Select your book cover to see a list of related content.

Index

Agra, India, 5
arches, 14, 15
architect, 9
brick, 12
building location, 5
building supplies, 10, 13
calligraphy, 14, 15
cars, 18, 19
clay, 20
colors, 6, 10, 12
dome, 14
elephants, 10
exterior, 6
factories, 18, 19
foundation, 10
gemstones, 12
guesthouse, 16
history, 8, 9, 10, 12, 13
Jahan, Shah, 8
Lahori, Ustad Ahmad, 9
leaders, 19
Mahal, Mumtaz, 8

marble, 6, 12, 13, 18, 20
mausoleum, 4, 12, 13, 16
minarets, 13
mosque, 16
name, 4
pollution, 18, 19
Qur'an, 14
red sandstone, 10, 17
reflecting pool, 7
shape, 14
size, 14, 17
stone, 10
visitors, 7, 18
wells, 10
workers, 9, 10, 12, 20
Yamuna River, 4, 5

The images in this book are reproduced through the courtesy of: Belikova Oksana, front cover; Igor Plotnikov, front cover (inset), background (throughout); Smarta, front cover (inset); Boedie_oetomo, icon (throughout); AlexAnton, pp. 3, 4; muratart, p. 6; Nicole Kwiatkowski, p. 7; Dinodia Photos/ Alamy Stock Photo, p. 8; Chughtai Museum/ Wikimedia, p. 9; Matyas Rehak, p. 10; AlexAnton, pp. 10-11; Vikram_B, p. 12; Rawf8, p. 13 (red sandstone); Vladyslav, p. 13 (brick); Bazancik/ Alamy Stock Photo, p. 13 (white marble); nstanev, p. 13 (gemstones); Freesurf, pp. 13, 23; atosan, p. 14; Prabhakarans12, pp. 14-15; Sunil Singh, p. 15 (inset); Uladzik Kryhin, pp. 16-17; ZUMA Press, Inc./ Alamy Stock Photo, p. 18; Pallava Bagla/ Getty Images, p. 18 (inset); Raicho, p. 19; Juergen Hasenkopf/ Alamy Stock Photo, p. 20; Richie Chan, pp. 20-21.